Singing Made Simple

Sean Jay

Published by Sean Jay, 2024.

SINGING MADE SIMPLE

First edition. March 2, 2024.

ISBN: 979-8224671915

Written by Sean Jay.

SINGING MADE SIMPLE

by Sean Jay MMus GGSMD

An easy, jargon-free guide for singers, answering questions regarding singing technique that you were always afraid to ask

- 1) Introduction

- 2) Diaphragmatic breathing – How to do it, why we do it, and how you know you've done it when you've done it

- 3) The Vocal Chords

- 4) The Resonating Chambers

- 5) Voice Placement

- 6) Vowel Shapes

- 7) A simple, yet highly effective vocal exercise to get you going

- 8) Supporting the breath using the 'tuck'

- 9) The intercostals: keeping the chest in the 'high' position

- 10) The musical line and making 'sense of the line'

- 11) Choosing repertoire

- 12) Final thoughts

Chapter 1 - Introduction

———

I HAVE HAD TWELVE SINGING teachers in my lifetime.

Some of them have been superb. Some of them have not.

My first 'singing teacher' was actually my piano teacher. In hindsight, he probably should not have been teaching singing at all, but I think he needed the money. At my first lesson, vocal technique was essentially ignored. He pointed in the general direction of my stomach, advised me to, "Breathe from there"... and that was it.

My second teacher was actually a trained singer, but I think she had somewhat lost the will to live. And she did nothing to sort out my technique either.

And so it continued, with each new teacher telling me that my previous teacher had taught me "nothing" and that they would teach me "everything!"

Time went by, and I found myself surrounded by professional singers, many of whom would speak in 'ivory tower terms' regarding the technical aspects of voice production. I've heard everything, including teachers advising me to "Sing from a dot here" (whilst pointing to their forehead), "Support the sound more!" (whilst failing to explain exactly what that entailed), through to "Keep in your box" (am I a dog?), "Imagine the sound coming out of the back of your head" (am I an alien?), and "Give it more of a sense of LINE, dear!".

When I began teaching singing, I discovered that a large number of students had had similar experiences with previous teachers. As such, I attempted to explain all the terminology that had confused me in my younger years, in a simple, easy-to-understand way. Using everyday analogies to illustrate vocal technique, I found that my students grasped the concepts with no difficulty, and consequently ended up singing better.

That is all a good singing teacher should do; enable you to sing better, with greater ease and more confidence.

This book puts into words my experiences as a singing teacher over the past thirty years, and will hopefully help not only those who are just starting out on their singing careers, but also those who have been performing for a long time, and are perhaps feeling a little lost in terms of vocal technique.

It should not be used as a one-stop-shop, but rather in conjunction with lessons from a great teacher.

Used with this book, I hope that you will be able to sing better, with ease.

Chapter 2 - Diaphragmatic Breathing

———

HOW TO DO IT, WHY WE do it, and how you know you've done it when you've done it

"Breathe from the diaphragm! If you want to sing properly you need to BREATHE FROM THE DIAPHRAGM!" To paraphrase one of my previous teachers.

"Right," I would say. "I'll get right on that..."

I didn't understand what it meant. I didn't understand how to do it. So I carried on doing what I had always done, using poor technique, in the hope that I would get away with it.

But eventually, as you climb the ladder of the professional music world, you realise that 'getting away with it' only takes you so far. Consequently, I found myself unable to sing certain songs. Technically, they were beyond me. And I knew that my poor technique was the root of the problem.

I have taught hundreds of students over the years. Some are complete beginners. Some are seasoned professionals. Nearly all of them had poor breathing technique when they first came to me.

At their initial lesson, I would always ask, "How can I help you?" Their reply would nearly always be, "I think I need to sort my breathing out."

To demonstrate their problem, they would then perform for me, and at the end of the song, I would say, "Yes. I think you do."

The question is, why? Why do we have to think about breathing at all? Surely breathing is something that we do everyday?

Right now (at the time of writing, at least!), I am breathing. You, the reader, are breathing.

Why isn't that enough? Why can't we just get on and sing, knowing that we can breathe, using our 'everyday breathing technique' and be done with it?

The analogy I use to demonstrate the importance of breathing is this: when you were at school, did you play the recorder? Most people did at some point, and even if you didn't, I am sure you will follow this analogy.

Imagine that you find your old school recorder in the bottom of a drawer somewhere and you think, "Oh! It's my old school recorder! I'll have a little toot!" You then put the recorder to your lips and give a very half-hearted blow into the instrument. Almost like a small, despondent sigh, which is only sounded by the breath itself, rather than a moan.

What would it sound like? The sound would be pretty pathetic. At best, it would be out of tune, unfocused, would lack incision, and overall would be pretty awful to listen to.

The reason? The recorder is a **wind** instrument. And whether you are talking about the recorder, the flute, the clarinet, the oboe, the saxophone, or even the trumpet, the trombone or the tuba; they are all **wind** instruments.

Wind instruments all have one thing in common, a law, if you like: that is that they need **pressurised** air being blown through them at all times in order to make a decent sound.

I am sure most of you have tried to play a trumpet at some point. It is very difficult even getting a small squeak out of the trumpet, never mind a decent, musical sound. That is because it requires a serious amount of **pressurised** air being blown through it to achieve a good sound.

Which leads us to the question; what sort of the instrument is the voice? The answer? Like the instruments listed above, it's basically a wind instrument. And, like the group above, it requires a certain amount of **pressurised** air being blown through it in order to make a decent sound. Unfortunately, the breathing technique that we use in our everyday lives (which, as you may now have noted, I call the 'everyday breathing technique'), which is fine for staying alive, sending emails, sending texts, sitting in the car; if we use that breathing technique *when we sing*, it's like picking up a wind instrument and giving it a very half-hearted blow.

In other words, the 'everyday breathing technique' is not enough. This is why we require the 'diaphragmatic breathing technique' instead. The question is; *how* do we do it, *why* do we do it, and *how* do you know you've done it when you've done it? Just pointing at the direction of someone's stomach and saying, "Breathe from there!" is not enough.

Therefore, for ease of learning, I have broken the 'diaphragmatic breathing process' up into five easy-to-learn stages. These are as follows:

1) The diaphragmatic breath itself (the actual breath in)

2) The tuck (which is used to pressurise the air and 'support' the voice)

3) The inhalation of the upper chest (involving the intercostal muscles)

4) The breath out (the retraction)

5) Keeping the chest in the 'high' position

Stage 1: The Diaphragmatic Breath

We begin with stage 1; the diaphragmatic breath itself. Firstly, I would like to discuss the 'why' regarding the diaphragmatic breath. We have already covered this to an extent with the wind instrument analogy. However, I would like to talk just a little more about this, albeit very briefly.

When we sing, we make a sound.

What is sound? Most people do not give this question a second thought. But quite simply, sound is **air** vibrating.

What is air? Air is small molecules of oxygen, that surround us. When we make those molecules of air vibrate, either by singing, clapping, or even playing a single note on a piano or other instrument, the air vibrates; in other words, the air molecules shake up and down, creating a sound. It is like dropping a pebble in a pond of water. The pebble makes the initial splash, and then the water waves radiate outwards from that initial 'impact' in concentric circles.

The same thing happens in the world of sound when you 'splash' the air in some way by making a sound. The vibrating air that is created by singing, clapping, or playing a note on an instrument radiates out from its original source and travels, in the shape of a wave, before hitting you squarely on the eardrum. Water waves and sound waves are very similar in shape; in other words, they are circular and they roll! Think of those large waves in Hawaii that surfers ride, rather than the water waves that a 4 year old might paint in class. And of course, the bigger the sound wave, the bigger the sound.

My job as a singing teacher, initially, is to take the sound wave that emanates from each of my students (which people hear as 'the voice') and make it bigger. Why? Because a small sound wave is not going to make much impact. A larger sound wave will. And in order to create that big sound wave, a **large** 'ocean' of air is going to be needed to be sucked into the lungs, and then pushed back out again as 'your voice'. Of course, this is only possible if you are using the diaphragmatic breathing technique. The 'everyday breathing technique' will not suffice.

Of course, it is the breathing apparatus in the human body that helps us achieve this process. We will now look at this in detail. There are only five things that you need to know about (at this stage) concerning the breathing apparatus and you will already be aware of them. These are:

1. The larynx
2. The windpipe
3. The lungs
4. The diaphragm
5. The stomach

Whilst the stomach is not technically 'part' of the breathing apparatus, it does get affected it by it, hence it's inclusion here.

The larynx resides in the throat. It's a simple tube, shaped a bit like an empty toilet roll, made up mainly of cartilage and muscles that are bound together by elastic tissues. It is usually referred to as the Adam's apple in men, or the voice box, for the simple reason that the vocal chords are located in the larynx. The larynx itself sits on top of the windpipe.

The windpipe (known as the trachea) is a longer tube, rather like an empty kitchen roll, that divides at the bottom like a road forking left and right, with one 'road' leading into the left lung, and the other into the right lung. Once inside the lungs, the roads 'break out' into branches, or bronchioles. For simplicity's sake, you have the upper branches, and the lower branches. It is worth using your favourite search engine at this point to look at some images of the larynx standing on top of the windpipe. Do this and you'll see exactly what I am talking about.

These branches are contained within the lungs. The lungs themselves are a bit like two spongy balloons, being as they both inflate, but are also rather rubbery in texture. Stretched out flat, they would occupy an area of nearly 100 metres! The left lung is slightly smaller than the right, on account of the fact that room has to be made for the heart. The right lung is made up of three sections, or 'lobes', whereas the left lung only has two.

Again, this is worth a look on your favourite search engine for images relating to this.

Below the lungs, we have the muscle known as the diaphragm. Most people do not even know what shape the diaphragm is, let alone what it does. When asking students, "What shape is the diaphragm?" I have, over the years, received hundreds of different answers. These have included "A squashed plum", or "A boomerang" and, most commonly, "A coat hanger." None of these answers are correct.

In fact, the diaphragm is shaped almost *exactly* like a parachute. Again, take a look online at the various images of the diaphragm. You will probably be shocked to discover that it is entirely different in shape to what you were imagining.

The diaphragm is stitched to the bottom rib, which gives it its parachute-shaped appearance. And it's big. In fact, the diaphragm is one of the biggest muscles in the human body. And like all muscles, it can move up and down. Being such a big muscle, you can imagine that, if you move the diaphragm up and down in any big way, there will be a noticeable physical change to your overall body shape. In the same way that, if you extend your arms fully over your head, there is a noticeable change to your physical appearance (looking now as if you are surrendering to something). So the same is true if you move the diaphragm fully. Keep that in mind as we continue.

Beneath the diaphragm, we have the stomach.

The question is; what do these things do? That is to say, in the context of singing, as opposed to any other function?

Put simply, the larynx contains the vocal chords. It also allows us to swallow, and prevents us from choking when we eat. Together with the windpipe, the larynx forms the top part of the 'breathing tube'.

The lower part of this 'breathing tube' is the windpipe, which simply acts as a passageway through which the air travels down into the lungs. In the same way that one uses a passageway to travel from one area of a house (such as the living room) to another (the kitchen), so the windpipe acts as a passageway through which the air travels into the body and out again. It is no more complicated than that.

The lungs are like two balloons. They simply inflate and deflate. The question is, how? In fact, the lungs do NOT move by themselves. They cannot. Why? Because they are not muscles! So what enables them to inflate and deflate? This actually leads us on nicely to the final question; what does the diaphragm do? What is it actually for?

Well, the first thing the diaphragm does is it provides a floor for the lungs to stand upon. Look back at the picture of the diaphragm you looked for earlier online, and you will notice a flat area on top of the muscle. The lungs stand upon this. This supports the lungs and prevents them from 'hanging' from the windpipe and sagging. In fact, without the diaphragm to stand upon, the lungs would strangulate, and you would suffocate! Look online for images of 'lungs on diaphragm' and you will see everything working together.

But... in modern life, where we *sit* on the sofa, we *sit* at the computer, we *sit* in the car, we *sit* at our desk... the human breathing apparatus barely has to move. And that's fine in our everyday lives! For most day-to-day events, a small amount of air, taken into the lungs, is all we need to keep functioning.

However, as stated previously, the 'everyday breathing technique' is not enough for singing. Instead, we require the 'diaphragmatic breathing technique'. The question is (as stated previously); how do you do it? And how do you know you've done it when you've done it?

Well, what we are talking about here is taking a BIG breath. When asked to do this, people often aren't very good at it. Usually, they puff their chest out, pull their stomach in, and their shoulders rise up and, as a result, they nearly throttle themselves.

To which I say, "Oh... that's actually the complete opposite to what you should be doing."

They then get upset and say, "Well, I am clearly incapable of taking a deep breath."

To which I say, "You'd take a deep breath if you *really* had to. Imagine you are on a big ship. The ship is sinking rather quickly. In order to get to safety, you need to swim underwater for a good minute or so to get to the emergency exit. Would you take a deep breath then? Of course you would! Anyone would. You would say, "Right! I'm going under." You would then fill your lungs to their full capacity. A one hundred per cent breath.

Now, a one hundred per cent breath is actually too much for singing. But the 'everyday breathing technique' only gives a thirty per cent breath, which is not enough. Therefore, we need something more. In fact, we need a breath that inflates seventy to eighty per cent of the lungs. Which is perfectly possible, when you consider we are ALL capable of a one hundred per cent breath in dire circumstances.

The question is (yet again)... how do we do it? And how do we know we've done it when we've done it?

The simplest way to do it is to breathe through the mouth to the open 'Ah' shape. This might seem completely and utterly obvious. But, my experience shows that, if you don't tell singers to do this, they do all sorts of weird things, including sucking the air through pursed lips, snorting, whistling and other peculiar methods.

Some singers will argue that they prefer to breathe through the nose when they sing (although, in reality, they actually don't in practice). This method may seem fine at first. Indeed, I have attended vocal workshops where the 'expert' has encouraged the participants to breathe through the nose. In truth, breathing through the nose does give you a deeper breath, because the breathing apparatus has to work harder to suck the air through the smaller holes. However, in practice, it takes far too long, tightens the muscles in the neck (putting unnecessary pressure on the vocal chords) and is no use if you are singing a fast song.

So... breathe through the mouth, initially to the open 'Ah' vowel shape (making the 'Ah' sound that you would if you were saying words such as *car*, *tar*, or *far*). Over time, you will probably breathe in to whichever vowel shape begins each line you are singing, but initially, where you are simply learning diaphragmatic breathing, use the 'Ah' shape.

Think of it like this:

We have all had conversations with people which, when ended, have required us to turn back to that person (usually as they are walking away) and say, "Ah! Just one more thing before you go..." That audible, intake of breath you take just before making that statement (usually because you remember with a slight surprise what the 'one more thing' is, and don't want them to miss it) is the breath you should be aiming for before you sing.

I have also been known to call this intake of breath the 'intake of pleasant surprise'; in other words, the medium-size, definitive breath you take when someone surprises you nicely. In doing this, there must be an **audible** intake of air. Breathing in silently (which I have heard choral directors demand of their singers in the past) is simply faking it, and does not actually do anything for you. Asking someone to sing, whilst breathing silently, is like asking a pianist to play the piano without moving their hands in any way at all. Utterly impossible.

Please note that it is the 'intake of *pleasant* surprise', not the intake of complete and utter horror. You do not wish to shock the body. Instead, it should be a gentle, yet DEFINITIVE breath.

This audible breath, taken before each and every line you sing, is all part of the singing process. And it is *this* breath that is the **first** sign that you have performed the diaphragmatic breath correctly. So the first sign that you have performed the diaphragmatic breath correctly, is the sound itself; the intake of pleasant surprise or, if you prefer, "*Ah*! Just one more thing..."

The second sign is a physical sign. As I explained earlier, the lungs stand on the diaphragm. However, the lungs do not stand *freely* on the diaphragm. In fact, the bottom of the lungs are actually *attached* or rather, stitched, to the diaphragm. The brain, which controls everything, sends a small electrical impulse to the diaphragm, which causes it to contract. You may have heard this expression before; the diaphragm contracts! Put simply, this means that the diaphragm *pulls down*. As a result, the lungs are stretched, or elongated, and the tiny valves at the end of the bronchioles (the branches of the lungs) open up. This creates a vacuum, sucking the air in... and that is how we breathe! It's so very simple.

Of course, the extent to which the diaphragm pulls down, determines how much air is taken in. If the diaphragm pulls down just a little bit, barely changing from it's usual parachute–like shape, we take in just a small amount of air. And this is how the diaphragm acts in our everyday lives, giving us just enough air to stay alive and do everything that modern life requires of us.

However, if you want a deeper breath, i.e. the seventy to eighty per cent required for singing, the diaphragm is going to have to work *much* harder. The good news is that it can pull all the way down to the lower ribs, where it ends up almost flat, like a pancake. It is **this** action that is required for great singing.

Of course, being such a big muscle (it's actually the third biggest muscle in your body), the diaphragm pushes all the organs and muscles directly below it *downwards*. The result of this is that the stomach is then pushed outwards. And it is the stomach being pushed out that is the one and only visible sign that you have performed the diaphragmatic breath correctly. You essentially end up looking pregnant with the breath!

Please note that the air is not going into the stomach. Some students have assumed this in the past. Rather, the stomach is pushed forwards and out of the way to make room for the descending diaphragm, which in turn, allows the chest cavity to expand, and the lungs to inflate.

Some of the singing teachers I was taught by spent a lot of time talking about feeling the air 'going into the back', or the sides, or down to the pelvic floor. Of course, there should be some feeling of movement in those areas. As you progress, you will feel this more and more. But mainly, the stomach, which gives less resistance (as there are no bones in the way), is the area that moves the most.

And that is it. It really is very, very simple. And no more complicated than that.

So how do we 'do' the diaphragmatic breath? You breathe in through the mouth to the 'Ah' shape, imagining either the 'intake of pleasant surprise' or 'just one more thing!'

And how do we know we've done it when we've done it? Because, as you breathe in, there should be 1) an audible intake of breath and 2) the stomach should expand outwards.

The best way to practice this is in front of a mirror. Be fairly strict with yourself. Ensure that your shoulders do not rise up and squeeze your neck, and concentrate ALL movement down towards the stomach area. At this stage, place as much emphasis upon the stomach area as you can, and as little on the chest as possible.

If nothing moves, lie down and try it. Even if you do manage the diaphragmatic breath successfully standing up, lie down and try it anyway. Place one hand on your stomach, take the breath, and watch your hand rise and fall. Because the core muscles (which help keep the upper body upright) are now relaxed, your diaphragm will be able to move up and down without restriction.

The good news is you can practice this anywhere! In the car, on the bus, in the office, or in bed. Whereas some vocal exercises require a degree of privacy, the diaphragmatic breath can be practiced anywhere.

Students ask me, "How long should I practice for?"

The answer really is, "How long is a piece of string?"

It is entirely dependent upon your own progress and where you are at as a singer. However, you need to get to the point whereby you do not really need to think about it. In other words, you should get to the stage whereby, when you are singing, the diaphragmatic breath kicks in, leaving you free to concentrate on other, more enjoyable things, like the songs themselves.

I would recommend setting aside ten or twenty minutes per day in the first week or so. Get yourself to the stage whereby it's almost entirely natural. After all, technique is something that is used almost subconsciously to achieve something of a technical nature, whether it be golf, tennis, or singing. When you are on stage, the last thing you want to be consciously thinking about is the diaphragmatic breath. Practice to the point at which it becomes completely natural. Then try singing a song, using the diaphragmatic breath, and see what difference it makes to your voice.

You yourself might not notice a change in the sound at first, owing mainly to the fact that we never hear our voices as they truly are. But those around you will. What you yourself should notice however is that singing is suddenly easier. You will be able to sing for longer, with greater ease, and the songs which have always defeated you might suddenly seem less difficult.

Stage 4: The Breath Out (the retraction)

You might be wondering if you have missed some pages in this book. By which I mean, you might have noticed that I have jumped from Stage 1 (the diaphragmatic breath) to Stage 4 (the retraction). Please note however that the order in which we do all five stages for breathing are not the order in which we learn them. Bear with me, and you will see why as we progress.

Essentially, Stage 1 is the first part of the breath in, and Stage 4 is the first part of the breath out.

Stage 4, the breath out, also known as the retraction, is quite simple to master. Having achieved the diaphragmatic breath in, causing the diaphragm to pull down and flatten, making the lungs inflate, you will now need to release it, and by doing so, the air will leave your lungs. However, it is important that this is done so in a steady and controlled manner.

Earlier in this chapter, I described the lungs as being like two balloons. That's a good analogy for the breath in. But it's not such a good analogy for the breath out, as balloons tend to deflate in all sorts of inconsistent ways. They either pop (leading to a sudden, explosion of air), or they release the air very, very slowly, if they are left lying around for weeks. This is not a good analogy for singing when you bear in mind that the voice requires **pressurised** air in order to make a decent sound.

Therefore, for the purposes of the breath out, or deflation, we are going to leave the balloon analogy alone, and we are going to consider something else that is inflatable (like the lungs), but when we deflate it, it is done so in a steady, controlled manner. The best analogy I can think of is an inflatable tire. Whether it be a car tire or a bicycle tire, tires are inflatable (like the lungs) but when they are deflated using the valve, the air is released in a slow, steady and controlled manner. And the hissing sound that a tire makes is the perfect sound to imitate when we are teaching our diaphragm to release the breath.

Try it now! Use Stage 1 to inflate, and then imitate the sound of a deflating tire, making a 'Ssssss' sound as you do so. Place your hand on your stomach (with your palm facing your tummy button) and feel your hand go out as you take the breath in, and then feel it go in as you breathe out. Imagine, if you like, that someone has a piece of string tied to the inside of your tummy button, and that piece of string is hanging out of your back. Imagine, as you breathe out, that someone is pulling the string *gently* from behind, pulling the stomach back in.

It is important to ensure that the 'Ssssss' sound you make is not too violent! You do not want to sound like an audience member hissing at the pantomime villain. On the other hand, ensure that it is not too pathetic either! Just remember the deflating tire sound, and copy that as you breathe out.

As you breathe out, keep the breath as steady and as straight as possible. Imagine a speedboat, crossing a lake; the water is completely smooth, which ensures that there are no bumps in the journey across the lake. Your breath out should be like this. Completely smooth, with no audible increases or decreases in pressure.

Most importantly, as you do this, use your hand as a gauge to ensure that you feel the stomach go out as you breathe in (the diaphragm pulling down flat like a pancake in the process), and then retract back slowly as you breathe out (your diaphragm returning to it's default parachute shape).

Very soon, this simple movement, this *diaphragmatic breathing technique,* will be what you use when you sing. And you will do it without even thinking about it, allowing for greater ease of singing, longer phrases, greater dexterity, and a much, much better sound. The next question is; how *is* the sound of the voice actually created? In other words, how does the air that we suck into the body by using the diaphragmatic breathing technique become our voice? This question leads us on to the next chapter, where we will look at the vocal chords.

Chapter 3 - The Vocal Chords

AS YOU ARE NOW AWARE, the breath is simply taken into the body when the diaphragm pulls down flat, elongating the lungs, and creating a vacuum. The air is released when the diaphragm returns to it's default, parachute-shaped position. If you are only breathing (in other words, if you are not speaking or singing), that is all that happens. However, if you wish to sing (or speak), other parts of the body are brought into play.

As you breathe out, the air passes quickly up the windpipe. At this point, the air molecules, whilst moving up the windpipe, are **not** vibrating. Bearing in mind that sound *is* vibrating air, the air in this instance is simply air moving up the windpipe and nothing more. If you are **not** speaking or singing, this is all that happens.

However, if you wish to speak or sing, something different occurs as the air passes through the body. Whilst breathing out, the air passes up the windpipe, and then reaches the larynx, at the top of which are contained the vocal chords. Again, check out images of vocal chords within the larynx online.

Look at these pictures and, as you do so, feel your own larynx. The vocal chords are actually located just inside the top of the larynx, stretched across it like two elastic bands. Therefore, comparatively speaking, the vocal chords are located almost at the back of the throat. In other words, they are quite close to the mouth and nasal cavities. This is important to understand, particularly when we discuss the matter of resonance in the next chapter. Don't worry about this for now, but simply bear in mind that the close proximity of the vocal chords to the mouth is important.

If you are able, take a look at the vocal chords online. There are some great videos of 'Vocal Chords in Action'.

As you will see, the vocal chords are 'V' shaped, and are made from very delicate folds of skin, which create ridges. Ridges are important in the world of sound.

For example, if you run your finger over the white notes on the piano (without actually sounding the notes themselves), there won't be much sound; perhaps a light clicking noise, and nothing more. However, if you run your finger over the raised black notes (again, without sounding the notes themselves), there will be a much louder sound. Rather like a frog's ribbit. Your finger, which impacts with the ridges of the black notes, creates this sound upon impact.

Similarly, imagine you are driving a car. The road is smooth. Then, you drive over a cattle grid. Inside the car, you and your passengers vibrate as you pass over the ridges of the cattle grid.

Exactly the same thing happens with the voice. However, rather than a finger (or a car!) 'passing' over your vocal chords, the air molecules pass over the ridges of the vocal chords.

If you are not speaking or singing, the vocal chords remain in the open, 'V' position. This means that the air actually passes *through* the vocal chords, and does not 'strike' the ridges. As a result, the only sound you make is that of breathing.

However, if we decide to speak or sing, the muscles around the vocal chords push them together the moment you decide to vocalise something. This process, whereby the chords come together is often referred to as 'engaging' the vocal chords. As a result, the air that passes through them now has to squeeze through the tight, barely discernible gap in the vocal chords that has been created. As this occurs, the air molecules *strike* the ridges of the vocal chords as they travel over them, and the air vibrates in the same way that we would vibrate as passengers in a car driving over a cattle grid.

What do you get when air vibrates? Sound!

And this is how the *initial* sound of the voice is made. Think of it as the initial spark.

The question is; how much sound does this process actually make by itself? In other words, how much volume is created by the vocal chords themselves?

The answer is; very little. In fact, if you were to talk to people using only your vocal chords and no other parts of the body (apart from the diaphragmatic breath, without which there would be little to no sound at all), your voice would be very thin, very reedy, and very weedy. Only those people standing right next to you would be able to hear you.

So the big question is: how do we take the small 'spark' of sound, that initial vibration that is created by the vocal chords... and make it bigger? Louder? Richer? The answer is *resonance*.

Chapter 4 - The Resonating Chambers

———

PERHAPS THE GREATEST mystery surrounding voice production is that of the resonating chambers.

Singers talk about the resonating chambers in the same way explorers speak of the Holy Grail. The question is, what are they, where are they, and how do we use them? And, more importantly, how do we transform the weedy, reedy vibration that is created by the vocal chords, and turn it into something fabulous?

The analogy I use is this: imagine you own an expensive acoustic guitar. We take a string off the guitar, give it to Superman, and ask him to hold it taught, so that the string is as tight as it is when it is attached to the guitar. We then pluck the string. What would it sound like? It would probably be rather pathetic. Like the vocal chords by themselves, the string would sound reedy, weedy, and would lack richness.

Thanking Superman for his work, we then take the string back, attach it to the guitar, tune it, and then strike the string. How does it sound now? It will sound as it should; rich, glorious, and full of tone.

The question is, why? The answer, naturally, is that the sound of the string resonates in the 'bowl' of the guitar.

But what does this actually mean? What actually happens physically?

Essentially; you strike the string. The air around the string vibrates, and radiates like a water wave, just like a pond when you throw a stone into the water, and the water radiates outwards (as a wave) from the initial 'splash' towards the edge of the pond.

Some of the air around the guitar string travels out into the room you are in, and is lost. But *some* of that vibrating air travels down, through the round hole of the guitar, into the 'bowl', where it *mixes* with the 'still' air that is naturally present. This creates a kind of 'snowball' effect.

What happens to a snowball when it rolls down a snowy hill? It gets bigger and bigger.

What happens to a whirlwind when it picks up more air? It becomes a tornado. What happens to a tornado when it picks up more air? It becomes a hurricane.

The same thing happens *in miniature* in the guitar's 'bowl'. Or, to give it it's proper title, it's **resonating chamber**. As previously stated, you strike the string on the guitar, and the air around the string vibrates outwards in a circular pattern. Some of that vibrating air travels into the guitar's resonating chamber, and mixes with the 'still' air that is naturally present. The 'still' air then begins to resonate and reverberate at the *same pitch* as the original guitar string. Consequently, there is now **much** more air vibrating. As a result, the sound is now bigger.

Every acoustic instrument on the planet has some type of resonating chamber, in which the initial sound vibrates, or reverberates, or resonates; all these words mean the same thing. A resonating chamber is simply a space in which vibrating air 'infects' or 'infuses' the still air, and becomes bigger, or snowballs. In a way, a resonating space is a place in which a small vibration goes viral, and becomes huge.

Think of a grand piano. Where do the strings vibrate, or rather, resonate? Obviously, they resonate inside the main body of the piano, before the sound then travels (in the shape of a wave) and hits you, the listener, squarely on the ear drum. The smallest grand piano (known as a baby grand) is just under five feet in length. The largest grand piano (known as a concert grand) is just over ten feet in length. Why do they make grand pianos that big? Because quite simply, the more air you have vibrating inside the case, the bigger the sound! With a concert grand, you have more chance therefore of competing with a symphony orchestra, or filling a large auditorium.

So... if every acoustic instrument on the planet has a resonating chamber, where are the resonating chambers for the human voice located? The answer? Inside your *head*.

The brain takes up two-thirds of your head, which is not inconsiderable. However, this does mean that there is a space of one-third that is technically 'empty'. This includes both the mouth, and the big space behind your nose, known as the nasal cavity. Again, check out 'human resonating chambers' online, and you will see this in all it's glory.

And, *if* you know how, you can encourage the small vibration that is created by your vocal chords to 'mix' with the still air that lies naturally in your mouth and nose, as it passes on it's journey through these chambers. As a result, the sound becomes bigger and rounder as it resonates in the head. Indeed, the pressurised air from the lungs 'mixing' with the still air in the resonating chambers can be like a miniature nuclear reaction inside the head... if you can do it.

The question is, how *do* you do it? How do you get the sound to resonate in the resonating chambers? The answer is... you already do! If you didn't, you would sound a bit like an EastEnd gangster from the 1960's, whereby the sound very much comes from the back of the throat. We all know people who talk like that, where the sound is very raspy, quite thin and has little tone. We also know people who use their resonating chambers in a very big way. Shakespearian actors for example, whereby the sound is rich and sonorous, and carries all the way to the back of the theatre.

But no matter to what extent you use your resonating chambers, you can always use them more! What we need therefore, are **specific** vocal exercises that 'hit' the right spots, and encourage the voice to resonate to the best of its vocal ability. I call these the resonating exercises, as they are somewhat different to the more athletic exercises that are sounded on more open vowels. They include:

1. Lip trills. Essentially, you pick a note and roll the lips to the "Brrrrrrrrrrr" sound as you do so. The "Brrrrrrrrrrr" sound is an elongated version of the sound that you make at the beginning of each of the words, "British Brown Bread".

2. The "NG" sound. This is the sound that you get at the end of any word which ends in "NG" and includes words such as "sung" and "lung" and "bung". You simply hold onto the "NG" sound and resonate upon it. Often, singers will 'siren' on this sound, sliding up and down between one note and another.

3. Humming. This has been used for hundreds of years to develop the voice.

The lip trills are discussed fully in Chapter 7, and you may, if you wish, jump forward to that chapter now, and take a look at them.

Chapter 5 - Voice Placement

I AM NOW ASSUMING THAT you have a better idea regarding how the initial sound of the voice is made.

A simple revision of the process:

The air is sucked into the lungs as a result of the diaphragm pulling them down and creating a vacuum. As the diaphragm pulls down and ends up flat like a pancake, it pushes all the organs and muscles below it downwards, which in turn pushes the stomach out. The stomach being pushed out is the one *visible* sign that you have done this correctly.

And the one *audible* sign that you have done this correctly is the 'intake of pleasant surprise' or 'just one more thing' rush of air that occurs as the breath is taken in. Remember; do not shock the body by overdoing this breath, but do not underdoit either by taking in too little. You are aiming for a positive, definitive action here.

As you allow the diaphragm to retract back slow and steadily under *your* control to its original, parachute shaped position, the air leaves the lungs and travels up the windpipe. The air then reaches your larynx where, should your vocal chords be 'engaged', it will pass over the ridges and vibrate, creating a small, reedy sound. This small sound will then enter (what is by comparison) the massive resonating space in your mouth and nasal cavity. The vibrating, pressurised air from the vocal chords then 'mixes' with the air in your resonating chambers, causing that air to vibrate also, making the sound bigger and richer.

Before shaping this sound into words, you must ensure that it is all 'brought forward.' For a couple of years, I had a singing teacher who consistently told me, "Bring the sound forward more, dear!"

I had no idea what she was talking about, so I would nod my head, carry on as I had before, at the conclusion of which she would say, "Yes, 'that's much better."

I highly doubt it.

Yet, looking back, I now realise that she was referring to voice placement. Singers talk about voice placement a great deal. Generally, when commenting upon a good voice, they will say, "The voice is nicely forward." Or conversely, if someone is having trouble, they will say, "The sound is a bit too far *back*."

But what does it mean? As ever with singing, it is actually terribly simple.

What they are referring to is where the voice *focuses* inside the head. To explain this, I use the following analogy:

You have no doubt, at some point in your life, been to the cinema. Most cinemas are shaped like a rectangular box, with four walls. And whilst it is rounder, your head (particularly when you think about the resonating chambers only) also has four walls, and is shaped somewhat like a box, albeit more circular.

When you go and see a film, you expect all the light and colour that is projected from the back of the cinema to focus upon the screen in front of you. You would not be impressed if the projectionist pointed the projector at the floor, or maybe half-way down the wall on the left hand side of the room. You would ask for your money back.

So the same is true for the voice. As you know, when you sing, the air rises up the windpipe, past the vocal chords, vibrates as a result, enters the resonating chamber where it picks up more air (which vibrates, making it bigger) and *hopefully* continues to travel forwards towards the mouth... but if the sound somehow gets stuck, and doesn't *focus* rightat the 'front' of the face (also referred to by some singers as the 'mask'), you might be accused of not 'bringing the sound forward' enough.

To demonstrate what I mean, simply sing the "Aah" vowel right now. Without hurting your voice, make it slightly ugly, almost like the sound an old witch in a pantomime would make. This is "Aah" as in the words cat, sat and mat, rather than car, tar and far. As you do this, you will 'feel' most of the sound is being made at the *back* of the mouth, or even down in the throat. In other words, the sound will be at the *back*.

Now sing the "Ooh" vowel quietly. This is "Ooh" as in the words too, loo, and boo. You will notice now that the sound appears to be focusing mainly at the *front* of the mouth. It is this sound which you should be aiming for when you sing.

Obviously the "Ooh" vowel is easy in this respect, the funnel-like shape of the lips focusing the sound at the front of the mouth as you sing. It is harder as the vowels become more open, and in no way would I want any readers of this book to end up creating peculiar vowels and distorted facial shapes as a result. In the end, every sound you make should be natural to you.

But be aware of the difference between the vowel shapes, and the different places that they resonate and then ultimately focus in the head.

Chapter 6 - Vowel Shapes

BY NOW, I HOPE YOU are very much aware of how the voice works. And how simple it really is.

Were I to be explaining *any* other instrument, we would now be finished.

Take the piano, for example, which has some (albeit vague) analogies with the voice.

Your fingers rise to strike the piano keys. This is similar to taking the breath in when you sing. It is the preparation of the note.

Your fingers move downwards to strike the piano keys. This is similar to the breath rising up out of the lungs, and up the windpipe.

Your fingers strike the piano keys and, in turn, the hammers inside the piano hit the strings, creating an impact in the air which creates sound. This is similar to the breath striking the ridges of the vocal chords and making a small, reedy vibration.

The strings of the piano resonate inside the main body of the instrument, or to give it its proper title, the resonating chamber. This is similar to the vibrating air which comes initially from the vocal chords before then resonating in the human resonating chambers. In both cases, the sound becomes bigger, richer, and fuller.

And with the piano... that's it! That's how it works. The sound escapes from the piano's resonating chamber, travels a few feet to your ears, and hits you on the eardrum. No further explanation of 'how the piano works' is really needed.

However, with the voice, there is an added complication that *no other instrument* has.

That added complication is words. The musical sound that emanates from us, which people hear as 'our voice', must be shaped into words. This is not something required of the piano, or the flute, or the violin, or the trumpet. It is solely peculiar to the voice. Even if you are just on stage, singing backing vocals to the "Ah" and "Ooh" vowels, you are still *shaping* the musical sound that's coming out of you into something.

Generally speaking however, when we sing, we sing fully-formed words. Words are made up of two things; vowels and consonants. When we sing, because of the elongated nature of the musical line (i.e. holding onto words when they are attached to a long note), an overemphasis should be placed upon the vowels. In fact, particularly when we are singing ballads, or any type of slow songs, you will find yourself singing and holding onto vowels for more than ninety per cent of the time that you are vocalising.

For example, when you sing the line, "I love you," you will use the vowel shapes "I" (for the word 'I'), "uh" (for the word 'love') and "ooh" (for the word 'you') for the large majority of the time that you are actually singing that line. Less time should be spent vocalising the consonants, although when you do sound the letter "l" at the beginning of the word 'love' and the "y" at the beginning of the word 'you', you should ensure that they are clean and crisp. Otherwise, your singing will become sloppy and inprecise.

As you are aware, there are five vowels in the English alphabet; a, e, i, o, u.

These five vowels, together with their phonetic variants (that is to say, the *way* in which we usually say them: ah, aye, ee, o, ooh) need to be well shaped by you, the singer. They are shaped naturally by the lips, the tongue, the soft palate and the jaw.

Badly shaped vowels can let you down. You might be able to breathe well, resonate fantastically... but if you shape the sound badly, falling at this final hurdle, everything you will have done before in terms of breathing, vocalising and resonating will have been a waste of time. So often, shaping the sound has been the issue that I have had to work very hard upon with my students.

One solution to finding the correct vowel shape is to get the student to *say* the word they are singing badly first. I ensure that they say it in the most natural way possible, whilst paying full attention to the shape of the vowel. They say it. Then sing it.

It is this part that always requires a second set of ears, and it is for this reason that I would always recommend that you find a great teacher who can work with you, and adjust the 'shape' accordingly.

Some of the greatest singers in the world **still** have singing lessons, even at the peak of their careers. Why? Do they still have things to learn? Whilst I would say that one never stops learning when it comes to issues regarding voice training, the main reason is so that they ensure that any bad habits (which can creep in at any point during a singer's life), which they may be unaware of, are gotten rid of. Often the shape of their vowels are the main problem. And because we often do not hear our voices 'as they really are', it takes a second set of ears, in the form of a good singing teacher, to correct the faults.

You can also record yourself, and listen back to the recording. As you do so, listen very carefully. You may find yourself pronouncing certain vowels in a way that you would never do when you are speaking, perhaps because you are putting on a voice, or are copying someone that you might have heard and admire. So play around with the *shape* of the vowel, aiming for the most open, yet natural sound that you can, record yourself again, and see if the sound has improved.

My third singing teacher out of the twelve that I had was very focused upon vowels. He would always say, "Singing is all about good, well-shaped vowels."

Well, the vowels are very important, of course. But one must ensure that the diaphragmatic breath is being performed correctly, and that the sound is resonating properly in the head, before one thinks about the vowels, hence the order in this book.

But ensure that, when you do shape the vowels, you do so in the clearest way possible.

If in doubt, say it, then sing it.

Record yourself.

And find a good singing teacher who will help you fix any peculiar vowel shapes you may have.

Chapter 7 - A simple, yet effective vocal exercise

THE LIP TRILLS (AKA The "Brrrrrrrrrs")

Often referred to as either lips trills, this exercise is one of the most widely used vocal exercises in the world. As stated previously, it is the sound that you get at the beginning of each of the words, '**Br**itish **Br**own **Br**ead', with an emphasis and elongation upon the 'Brrrrrrr' sound, using the LIPS! Do not use the tongue! You will only cheat yourself.

If you stand outside the dressing room door of any great singer, and they have been well-taught, you will generally hear them using this sound to warm up with. The question is why? There are three reasons and they are three of the most important aspects regarding vocal production. They are as follows:

1) Breath Connection:

The lip trills act as a 'breath connection' exercise. For many years, before I trained properly, I would hear singers talk about 'breath connection.'

They would make comments such as, "I heard Sarah sing the other day. She has the makings of a good instrument... but the breath just wasn't connected to the voice!"

I am sure you yourself have attended concerts or gigs, or heard singers on television who are reasonably good, but there is just something missing in terms of the sound itself. Usually, it is due to a lack of breath connection.

But what exactly is breath connection? The analogy I use is this: when I was at music college, my Professor of Singing would say, "The breath is the fuel for the voice." My question to you is; what else do we have in the physical world that uses fuel? The answer is, obviously, cars.

Whether you can drive or not is irrelevant to this analogy, but imagine the following: as you know, with most cars, the engine is at the front, and the fuel tank is at the back. You get into your car in the morning, and flick the ignition. The fuel is pumped, from the fuel tank, down the fuel line, to the engine at the front. The fuel *connects* to the engine. And what does the engine do? It starts! In fact, most people who imitate engines, make the 'Brrrrrr' sound, which is quite helpful regarding this analogy.

Imagine a different situation now: you get into your car in the morning, you flick the ignition, and for some reason or another, usually because the fuel tank is empty, or the fuel pump doesn't get the fuel to the engine *at the correct pressure*, the fuel doesn't reach the engine. Or to put it simply, the fuel does not *connect* to the engine. What happens? Very little. The engine either doesn't start, and if it does, it generally splutters and then stalls.

Exactly the same is true of the human voice. Remember that the voice is a *wind* instrument, and it requires **pressurised** air in order to make a decent sound. Like the car, you must ensure that, once you have taken the diaphragmatic breath into the lungs (or, for this example, the fuel tanks), that breath then reaches the 'engine' (the vocal chords and resonating chambers) at the correct pressure.

And how can we be certain as singers that we are getting the breath from the 'fuel tanks' to the 'engine' at the correct pressure? The answer is simply by whether or not we can do the 'Brrrrrrrs.'

Essentially, the lip trills act as your pressure gauge. If you are breathing properly, and the air is leaving the lungs at the correct pressure, you will be able to perform the lip trills correctly. If you are not, nothing will happen.

Please be sure that you actually *feel* your breathing apparatus (stomach, diaphragm and lungs) **driving** the lip trills! It is no use just using the air in your mouth. Breath connection is a conscious, physical connection between the lungs and the rest of the voice. The feeling is quite subtle, but it is there. And the main way to be able to tell that it *is* there is a successful lip trill.

You may have trouble with this exercise at first. If you really, really cannot get the lips moving at all, you can put your index fingers in the dimples of your cheeks and try again. You should find that it works. This will then enable you to get used to the *sensation* of the lip trills, which is better than not doing it at all.

Using the fingers in this way is cheating, to a certain degree. However, when we first learn to ride a bike, we usually use stabilisers. Of course, the *most* important skill to master when riding a bike is that of balance. Using stabilisers takes away the need for that skill and you could say that, as such, they defeat the object of the exercise. However, they do enable you to get used to the feeling of riding a bike; of using the handlebars, the pedals and the brakes. This in itself is useful. You can then take away the stabilisers once you are used to the *sensation* of riding the bike. The same is true of using your fingers to facilitate the lip trills. It takes away the initial need to pump the right amount of air through the body, but at least it gets you used to the sensation.

In conclusion, do try the exercise using the breath and the lips by themselves.

2) Stimulation of the Resonating Chambers:

The second reason why the 'Brrrrrrrs' or lip trills are so good as a vocal exercise is because they help to stimulate your resonating chambers. "That's nice," I hear you say. "What on earth does that mean?!"

When you decide to study any other instrument, whether it be piano, guitar, violin etc., do you need to grow the trees for the wood first? Cultivate the strings? No! The instrument comes ready made.

The voice, however, needs to be grown organically, in the same way that you would grow a plant. Growing a plant requires some work, in terms of watering, plant-food and sunlight. Bearing in mind that your lungs, larynx, vocal chords and resonating chambers are made up of organic tissue, they require water, food and the like, but when you are building the voice up through vocal training, the voice needs something extra. Hence the need for vocal exercises.

Every vocal exercise does something different for the voice, building up different parts of it, in the same way that pulling weights in different ways in the gym builds up different muscles.

As we saw in Chapter Four, the voice has natural resonating chambers in the mouth and nasal cavity. However, before we begin serious vocal training, the voice may not be resonating, or rather vibrating to it's full capacity in those spaces.

It needs encouragement to do so! It's almost like saying to the voice, "Look... there's all this space inside my resonating chambers. Could you use them more please?"

The voice replies, "What space? I can't *feel* it."

You then do a lip trill. The sound *vibrates* inside the mouth, and the voice says, "Oh yes! I can feel that space! I shall use it more often." It is like removing a false roof in a large hall, discovering a dome above it, singing in the space, and finding that the sound is suddenly far more resonant and satisfying. Rather like singing in the shower, but on a bigger scale.

The more you use the lip trills, the more the voice gets used to resonating in the head. As a result, the natural resonance of the voice increases. Remember; sound *is* air vibrating. The more air that vibrates, the bigger the sound. Therefore, if you add *more* vibrations to the air as it passes through the instrument (which in this case is your body), the sound will be bigger, richer and fuller.

The concept of resonance, and increasing resonance vocally is, I believe, one of the hardest things to teach in terms of singing. I remember when I was first in training, at the age of 14, and I would talk with older, more experienced singers, who would talk about resonance all the time. To some extent, they would speak of it as if it were the holy grail, available only to the most privileged. As a result, I *thought* I probably knew what it was, but in truth I was not entirely sure.

Essentially, however, it is the **tone** of your voice. When you sing to your audience, what is the first thing you want them to say? I expect you would like them to say, "Good voice! Great sound!"

My question to you is, when they make this comment, what aspect of your voice are they referring to? You might think it is the volume. But it isn't. First and foremost, it's the tone. The overall sound.

You might have a loud voice, which might seem impressive to some people. But if the tone is ugly, people are not going to want to listen to it for very long. In fact, some of the most fabulous singers I know do not have the world's biggest voices. But the tone and quality of their voices are to die for.

Coming back to the lip trills, remember that they are, first and foremost, a breath connection exercise. But they are secondly a resonance exercise.

Used regularly, the 'Brrrrrrs' will enhance the natural tone and quality of your voice.

3) Voice Placement:

The final way in which lip trills help the voice is through the concept of voice placement. In other words, the 'Brrrrrrs' help to 'bring the sound forward'.

This concept has already been discussed in Chapter 5. Remember that you want all of the vibrating air that makes up your voice to *focus* at the front of your mouth, like a projectionist in the cinema who aims all the light and colour that emanates from a projector down onto the screen at the front.

Usually, when we first wake up in the morning, the sound of our voice is often 'at the back' of the mouth. We sound croaky, and it can take a while for the voice to warm up, before it really starts resonating.

Doing lip trills however can hurry that process along, particularly first thing in the morning. Just a few minutes doing the 'Brrrrrrs' can do wonders, and get the voice focusing at the front of the mouth. Which is exactly where you want it. It will stay there for the rest of the day, until you go to sleep at night. When we sleep, all the muscles relax, and the tautness which is derived from vocal exercises and singing songs, loosens. The spring uncoils. It is for this reason that we have to warm up everyday. Essentially, we are tightening the spring.

Some singers find warming up a tedious affair. Some enjoy it. Whatever the case, it has to be done. Singing without warming up is like running a marathon with little to no preparation. It can be done, of course; but after a while, the body begins to rebel in all sorts of horrible ways.

In conclusion therefore, the 'Brrrrrrrs' are an excellent exercise, on account of the fact that, whilst being very simple, they do huge amounts for the voice.

They connect the breath, stimulate the resonating chambers, and help with good voice placement.

The question is, how to practice them? Actually, you can do whatever you like. You can simply slide up and down a scale. It doesn't have to be particularly musical either. But that might not excite you, so my suggestion would be to 'Brrrrrr' along to your favourite songs. You may feel ridiculous, but it will do you a lot of good. Once you feel sufficiently warm, try singing the same songs... and see what a difference it makes.

Remember that the improvements to our voices are usually heard by those around us *first*. Because so much of the sound when we sing (and speak) is made in the head, in between your ears, we always get a somewhat distorted impression of what we really sound like. Yes; that is the reason we sound so different when we hear ourselves recorded.

Instead, what you should notice first, is that singing simply becomes easier. I have had many students report back to me that, once they have got their diaphragmatic breathing in order, and the 'Brrrrrrrs' are working nicely, they find that singing for longer, with less fatigue, is simply easier.

Chapter 8 - Support!

SUPPORTING THE BREATH using the 'tuck'

"Support the breath!"

"Support the voice!"

"Support the sound!"

Phrases I've heard for years, barked out by singing teachers, choral directors and conductors.

Their students often nod, as if to say, "Yes, ok. I will support the breath/voice/sound." In reality, I reckon most think, "I guess they want me to breathe more," or "I have no idea what you are talking about, so I will just nod my head and pretend that I do, in order to get you off my back."

Some students have come to my studio, thinking that 'support' is the diaphragmatic breath. But it's not. Support is actually what you do to the breath *after* you have taken it. And we use a physical technique called 'the tuck' to achieve it.

The tuck does two things for the voice. It supports the voice (as stated above) but it *also* pressurises the air. Remember; the voice is an organic wind instrument. It needs pressurised air being blown through it in order to make a decent sound. The tuck helps with that pressurisation.

Let's talk about support first. With your knowledge from this book, you are now aware that the voice is, to all intents and purposes, an upright, physical object. By which I mean, we have (starting at the physical 'bottom' of the voice) the stomach, on top of which we have the diaphragm, on top of which stand the lungs, on top of which we have the windpipe, on top of which we have the larynx, at the top of which we have the vocal chords, on top of which we have the resonating chambers.

Look around the room you are currently sat in. I have no doubt you can find several upright, physical objects. The room I am writing this book in contains an upright piano, some stereo speakers, and a lamp, as well as other objects. The piano is supported by the floor. The lamp is supported by it's stand, and the stand is supported by the floor. The speakers are placed up on stands. Again, like the lamp, the speaker stands are supported by the floor.

The floor is solid. Wooden flooring, laid upon concrete. I am sure that the floor of the room you are reading this book in is also good and solid. Stand on the floor. Do you have trouble standing upon it? No! The floor supports you and stops you falling over.

But... have you ever been on a bouncy castle? What is difficult about trying to stand on a bouncy castle? You are not supported! The floor is spongy. It moves. You wobble around, trying to keep your balance.

Have you ever tried to stand on a mattress or maybe a sofa, whilst hanging a picture up behind it? I'm sure you found the process quite difficult as the mattress or sofa upon which you were standing constantly moved around under your feet. You would have been unsupported.

As previously stated, your voice is an upright, physical object. It 'stands' upon the diaphragm, underneath which you have the stomach.

Take the diaphragmatic breath and then use the retraction to release the air (Stage 1 and Stage 4). As you release the air, prod your stomach and surrounding area with your finger. How does it feel? Is there some feeling of 'give'? Does it wobble slightly? Does your voice fluctuate as you prod yourself? If so, your voice could be said to be 'unsupported' in the same way that any other upright object in the physical world would be, were it placed on a wobbly, squelchy surface.

Even if you are not prodding your stomach, I am sure you can now see how, even with the slightest physical movement (a slight move to the left or the right, for example), your voice will wobble if the foundations beneath it are not secure. And I am sure that, when you sing, you do not stay entirely motionless, like a statue. Indeed, even taking the diaphragmatic breath itself causes the body to move, creating ripples which can unsettle the rest of the instrument if you do not 'tether' it down before vocalising.

We therefore need to do something about this. We need to 'support' the voice as an upright physical object. We therefore use the 'tuck'.

In explaining what the 'tuck' is and how to do it, I am now going to talk about the second reason why we use the 'tuck'. I will then return to the notion of 'support' afterwards.

The second reason that we use the 'tuck' is that it pressurises the air. As stated earlier, I am hoping that you are now feeling comfortable with the diaphragmatic breath. Technically, this gives you a larger quantity of air than you would have otherwise; but now we need to pressurise that air. Whilst the retracting diaphragm *does* place some pressure upon the lungs, it is not enough. We need to increase the pressure.

Why is this? The analogy I use is as follows: I am sure that at some point, you have used a lilo, or an inflatable bed to lie on whilst at the beach or the pool.

Imagine this: you are on holiday, at the beach. You are lying on your lilo, out on the water. The sun starts to go down, so you paddle back to shore. You need to deflate the lilo entirely, so that it will fit in the back of your small hire car. However, because you are on holiday, you are not in any rush. So you pull the 'plug' out of the top of the lilo, and allow it to deflate of its own accord. You go off to the beach bar, grab a drink, and then return to the lilo an hour later. It has completely deflated with no physical help from you.

In this instance, how does the air 'leave' the lilo? Simply put, for the first second or so, when you pull the plug out, the air leaves quickly. But within two or three seconds, the pressure decreases, and the air leaves more slowly, until the lilo is completely deflated. As such, 99% of the air leaving the lilo could be said to be **unpressurised**. If you were to somehow attach a musical wind instrument to *that* air flow, you might get one or two decent notes out of it for the first second or so... but then, as the pressure decreases, the sound would be awful.

Now imagine this: You are on a daytrip at the beach. You are lying on your lilo, out on the water. The sun starts to go down, so you paddle back to shore. You then discover that it is actually much later than you thought it was. You also have an important engagement to get back to but... despite being in a rush, you still need to deflate the lilo entirely, so that it will fit in the back of your small car. So you pull the plug out of the top of the lilo, and do what to it?

Some of my students respond with 'sit on it!' That would actually be too violent and may cause the lilo to burst. Rather, you apply *constant* pressure with your hands to the main body of the lilo, until it has deflated. As such, 100% of the air leaving the lilo could be said to be **pressurised**. If you were to somehow attach a musical wind instrument to *that* air flow in that situation, you would get a consistently good sound.

Your lungs are like two lilos. If you take the diaphragmatic breath and then just let it go again, that is rather like the lilo that is allowed to deflate of its own accord. As such, your air flow could be described as being **unpressurised**. Bearing in mind that the voice is a wind instrument and requires pressurised air being blown through it, this is not what you want.

Therefore we need to do something about it. But what?

Well... you could take your hands and, in the same way that you press down lightly on the lilo to pressurise the air as it deflates, so you could do the same thing with your stomach.

How? Take the diaphragmatic breath. Your stomach will expand as you do so. Now lock your hands together in front of you, and place them up against your tummy button. Now pull your arms towards you and 'pull up' slightly, as if you are performing a lower-placed version of the Heimlich manoeuvre on your stomach. As you do so, you will pull the stomach muscles up against the flattened diaphragm. Muscles exist in one of two states; flaccid or flexed. Your bicep, for example, is usually flaccid. But if you squeeze it between your forearm and your shoulder, the bicep flexes. In the same way, if you use your hands and arms to pull your stomach up towards the diaphragm, whilst the fully inflated lungs are pushing down on it, the diaphragm will flex as it is squeezed between the two.

If you then ensure your arms continue to exert pressure on the stomach (which in turn, continues to exert pressure on the diaphragm and the lungs), the effect is similar to a deflating lilo which you apply constant pressure to. In this event, the air will be **pressurised**, which is exactly what you want.

However, the idea of singing in this way, whilst keeping your hands continually on your stomach, is ridiculous. Nobody in their right mind would do this. However, the *concept* is correct.

Whereas a lilo has no external muscles of its own to help it deflate, the human voice as a whole is different. By which I mean, we have the abdominal muscles which, once you have taken the diaphragmatic breath, you use to pull your stomach in with (as you did with your arms previously), or rather, you *tuck* your stomach muscles in, hence the name.

Essentially therefore, you should be aiming to take the diaphragmatic breath, which causes the stomach to expand outwards. Once inflated, you then should *gently* pull the stomach muscles back in towards the body, ensuring that, as you do so, you do not push all the air up into your chest. Please note that the tuck is not a crucifying kick in the stomach! All you are looking to do with it is to 'lock' the mechanism.

By doing this, and keeping the pressure on the diaphragm as you deflate the lungs, the air will remain pressurised. Which is exactly what you need.

But why does the tuck 'support' the voice? Again, take the breath and, without doing the tuck, let it go again. As you deflate your lungs, prod your stomach. You will feel that it is spongy and that there is plenty of 'give'.

Now take the breath again, but this time use the tuck. As you do so, prod your stomach. You should notice that the muscles are considerably firmer. Now let the air go but, as you do so, keep the stomach muscles flexed (in other words, keep tucking) and continue to prod your stomach. It should remain firm as you release the air. As such, you will be pressurising the air, but now, the muscles 'underneath' the voice are solid and firm. Therefore, your voice can be said supported!

What actual difference does this make to the voice? The best way to tell is to sing something. Record yourself if you can, even if you simply use your phone. Make two recordings; one without the tuck, and one with the tuck. You should notice that, with the tuck, the following occurs:

- The voice is more in tune

- The sound is more focused

- The tone is better

- Everything feels easier

Overall, the voice should simply sound more supported! I have tried for years to think of a better word than 'support.' I cannot. Support does exactly what it says on the tin.

Constantly engaging the stomach muscles in this way takes all the strain off the larynx, and allows the vocal chords to operate freely. This freeing up of the vocal chords then allows them to show you what they can really do. If you originally placed the 'strain' of singing upon your voice box, you probably became tired rather quickly.

The tuck 'takes the strain' off of the vocal chords, and instead places the pressure upon the stomach muscles. You may find that you come off stage with a slight ache in both your back and your stomach. Do not worry. These muscles are very strong and recover within seconds. And it goes without saying that it is far better to put this particular muscle set under strain, rather than the very delicate muscles around the vocal chords.

Some singers even squeeze their buttocks together, in order to 'belt' the sound out! That is perfectly acceptable. Anything below the line of the diaphragm is fair game, in terms of supporting the voice.

One word of warning. As is always the case with placing any kind of physical tension upon the body, you must ensure that the tuck does not creep up the body towards the throat! Some of my students have performed the tuck with such force, that their entire bodies have become tense. You do not want that. You must ensure that all tension is confined to the stomach area and everything below, whilst ensuring that your feet are planted firmly on the ground, six inches apart, with your knees unlocked.

Using the tuck 'rebalances' the voice. When some of my students begin their vocal training, the 'sound' of the voice noticeably stems from the throat.

Once I have taught them the art of diaphragmatic breathing together with the tuck, the area from which the voice originates, shifts. They come to realise that the voice can and should be *driven* from the bottom of the stomach, rather than yelled from the throat.

As such, it is important to realise that supporting the voice is not just a physical act; it is also psychological. Students realise that, rather than being just a noise that emanates from the vocal chords, the voice *is* air, pressurised and supported by the stomach muscles, which is then pushed up the windpipe. That pressurised, supported air then vibrates as it passes over the vocal chords, and resonates in the head (mixing with the 'still' air that naturally sits in the mouth and nasal cavity), is shaped into various words using vowels and consonants, and leaves the body via the mouth.

This feeling becomes second nature over time and becomes the only way to sing properly.

No doubt you are now thinking, "So I have to breathe... then tuck... and only then can I sing. That's a lot of things to think about before I even sing a note!"

Of course it is. But I recommend beginning slowly. Treat the diaphragmatic breath and the tuck as two separate actions at first. Think of them as two railway carriages, which are on the same piece of track, but are a distance away from each other. Then, gradually bring them together.

At first, you should practice 'Breath... then tuck'. Then bring them together slowly, the gap between the breath and the tuck becoming shorter, so that it eventually becomes the 'Breathtuck.' The 'Breathtuck'. All one smooth motion.

Obviously, be sure not to tuck *whilst* you are taking the breath, otherwise the stomach muscles will get in the way of the descending diaphragm. Rather, the tuck should *dovetail* the breath, once the diaphragmatic breath has been taken fully.

It will feel weird at first. It may feel like a lot of hard work. But your voice will suddenly find itself capable of doing things it couldn't do before.

The sound will be much improved. Songs that you thought were beyond you technically will suddenly seem much easier. You will make sounds that you have never heard your voice make before.

Of course, you will then probably forget to do it and will think, 'Why is my voice not sounding as good? And why does my throat feel tired?' And then you will remember, 'Ah. It's because I have forgotten to tuck.'

Support the breath!

Support the voice!

Support the sound!

Now you know how and why.

Chapter 9 - The Intercostals

<hr>

THE INTERCOSTAL MUSCLES: keeping the chest in the 'high' position

As you are aware, I break the breathing process down into five stages. So far, we have learnt three of them.

Stage 1 is the diaphragmatic breath itself. Stage 2 is the tuck. And Stage 4 is the retraction of the diaphragm.

This leaves us with two more stages. These include Stage 3 whereby we engage the intercostal muscles. And Stage 5, which encourages us to keep the chest in the high position.

A number of my singing teachers have placed a great deal of emphasis upon the intercostal muscles. They are very important, both in terms of breathing and singing, because they are the little muscles that are located in between the ribs. We have two sets of intercostals; external and internal.

When you breathe in, the external intercostals flex. By doing so, they 'lift' the ribs off the lungs a little, and allow the lungs more space to inflate. When you breathe out, the internal intercostals come to life, and push down on the ribs, bending them inwards, allowing the lungs to deflate.

Stage 3 works in conjunction with Stage 1, the diaphragmatic breath. Whilst you must emphasise at first sinking the breath down as low as you can, ensure that, once you have mastered the expansion of the stomach, you do not neglect the chest cavity.

Practice as follows: take the diaphragmatic breath. Now add the tuck. Now take another small breath *on top* of the initial diaphragmatic breath you have just taken. You should notice that the ribs move outwards. What has happened is that the external intercostals have flexed fully. By doing this, they allow more air into the lungs, giving you the desired 80 per cent breath for singing.

You should then aim to do this 'smaller breath' as part and parcel of the diaphragmatic breath, rather than two separate breaths, which would be ridiculous. Start by sinking the air down as low as you can, but then, as you engage the stomach muscles for the tuck, continue to breathe over the tuck. The whole process may sound complicated but in truth takes less than a second.

Now breathe out, keeping the pressure on using the tuck, and allow the diaphragm to retract back to it's original parachute shaped position. You may notice at this point that your chest begins to 'collapse' or sag. This leads us to the final stage.

At this point, you must use Stage 5, and keep the chest in the 'high' position. To do this, you must physically and consciously keep the back muscles and external intercostal muscles engaged as the internal intercostals attempt to bring the ribs down on the lungs. We are all capable of puffing our chests out when we need to, and this is no exception.

When you are nearly out of air, you should find that your stomach is flat and your chest is still in the high position. You may look like you are posing as a superhero. And that would be the correct physical position to end up with.

Keeping the chest in this position also enables the next breath that you take to be easier. The ribs are being kept off the lungs, allowing them to expand more easily. As such, any subsequent breaths you take can almost be regarded as 'top-up' breaths. Rather like driving a car when you go on a long journey, you top-up the petrol tank at each gas station, not knowing when you will get a chance to do so again.

No matter how long the musical line (or journey) is, whether it be four notes long or four bars long, you should always precede it with the breathing process I have described in this book.

The first breath at the beginning of a song (or after an instrumental break) will always require the largest intake of air. After that, try and think of every subsequent breath as topping up the first breath.

Take your time learning this breathing process:

- Stage 1: The Diaphragmatic Breath

- Stage 2: The Tuck whereby we support the voice as a whole and pressurise the air

- Stage 3: Engage the intercostal muscles allowing the ribcage to expand

- Stage 4: Allow the diaphragm to retract back to it's original position, deflating the lungs

- Stage 5: Keep the chest in the high position and do not allow the ribcage to collapse

Ask someone to watch you as you do all five stages. Ask them what it looks like to them. They will probably say, quite simply, "You are breathing from down there," whilst they point at your stomach.

As I stated at the beginning of this book, my first singing teacher pointed at my stomach and told me to, "Breathe from there." That was it. No other explanation was given.

The problem is, if you don't explain to students *precisely* what that means and how to do it, they will never, ever understand the mechanics of what is required.

I hope that, rather than confusing you utterly, these descriptions go some considerable way towards explaining exactly what is required of you breathing-wise when you sing.

Chapter 10 - The Line

THE MUSICAL LINE AND making 'sense of the line'

Now we move on to the way in which we actually sing. In other words, the delivery of the musical line. And making sense of that line. Which are actually two separate things.

The musical line:

Students ask me, "What is the musical line?" I give them the following analogy:

A director might ask an actor, "Can you give me that line again?" or, "Can you read that phrase again?" A line in English (or indeed, any language) is made up of words.

In music, we also talk about 'the line', but here we are referring **not** to a line of words, but a line of notes.

And unless stated otherwise, the line of notes that you are given should always be played (or sung) smoothly. You are probably familiar with the Italian phrase that is used in music to describe smooth playing or singing. It is legato.

When playing the piano, a line of notes are usually delivered smoothly by the pianist who will use good fingering technique, coupled with judicious use of the sustain pedal.

When we sing, we must also ensure that we sing the musical lines of notes smoothly. How do we do this?

Everything I have taught you in this book so far has been working towards creating a smooth legato line when you sing. Think about it: you take the breath in, and then exhale. As you do so, a long stream of pressurised air is pushed up the windpipe, past the vocal chords, into the resonating chambers and out the mouth. As such, you are already delivering a long 'line' of smooth, unbroken air.

However, when we sing, that air (now vibrating as a result of passing over the engaged vocal chords and resonating in the mouth) needs to be shaped into words. Specifically, vowels and consonants.

Without varying the pitch, sing the following line on a single note of your choosing:

"I think I love you!"

To begin with, sing it in a short, staccato-like way. You will probably sound like a robot.

Now, using all the correct breathing procedures, try again, but sing it as smoothly as you can.

As you do this, you should try and join all the notes up, ensuring that there are no gaps in the musical line. You should sound less like a robot, although singing it all on one note won't help. So alternate the pitch. It should sound better, but perhaps not as good as you would like it to be.

How can we improve this?

Firstly, try just singing the vowels of "I think I love you," so you end up singing something like this:

"Iy ee iy uh ooh"

Join all the vowels together, ensuring that there are no gaps between them. Technically, all that should really be moving is the mouth (asides from the breathing apparatus which powers the voice) as you change from one vowel shape to another.

No doubt you will be quite pleased with the sound you are making. It should sound smooth and resonant. However, you cannot just sing vowels, as lovely as they are. We need to put the consonants back into the line, in order for the words to be heard properly.

However, as we do so, be aware that it is the line of vowels that creates the beautiful musical line. You do not want to 'cut' that smooth line of sound any more than you have to.

Say all the consonants in the alphabet out loud to yourself. Say them phonetically; in other words, as they generally sound when you use them to create words, rather than the way in which a child might recite the alphabet. As you say them out loud, really focus upon **where** the sound is being made. In other words, is the sound of the consonant being made at the front of the mouth? Or somewhere else?

'B' (as in 'banana') is made at the front of the mouth, using the lips. 'C' is dependent upon which word it is being used for. If it is 'C' as in 'cake', then the sound is a glottal one, made in the throat. 'D' (as in 'duck') is made at the front of the tongue. 'F' (as in 'fried') is made at the front of the lips. And so on.

Run through them all. You will notice that, aside from some glottal sounds, most of the consonants are created at the front of the mouth, using the lips, the tongue, and the jaw. This is good news, as it enables us to keep the overall focus and sound of the voice *at the front of the mouth/ face at all times.*

Going back to "I think I love you", the first consonant we technically encounter is the 'th' sound at the beginning of 'think'. However, there is something else that we have to consider before this, and that is the diphthong that occurs as a result of the word 'I' at the start of the line.

A diphthong (literally meaning 'two sounds' in Greek), refers to two adjacent vowel sounds which occur within the same syllable. Say the word 'I' to yourself. You will no doubt be aware of the 'i' vowel. But there is something else there also, just at the end of the sound. It is the letter 'y.'

This can create a problem, for the simple reason that, in order to create the 'y' sound at the end, we need to close the mouth down somewhat. Whereas the 'i' sound is very open, and very close to the 'ah' shape, so the 'y' is used to shape the vowel also. Technically, this should occur *at the very last moment*. Do it too soon, and you will end up singing something akin to, "iiyyyyyyyyyyyy". As such, your mouth will spend most of the time closed, whilst you resonate on the 'y' sound, rather than the 'i.' I have even heard famous singers fall into this trap. As a result, the sound is never as good as it could be.

You should, as much as possible, always aim for the most *open part* of the vowel. Meanwhile, the other sounds around it (be they diphthongs or consonants) will then go towards creating the rest of the word you are vocalising. The most open part of the vowel will give you the sound you want. In this instance, you should therefore be aiming for, "iiiiiiiiiiiiiiiiiiiyy", with as little time spent on the second part of the sound as possible. Of course, as is always the case, do not go to the other extreme, whereby you leave the 'y' sound out all together, or else your singing will lack distinction and focus.

Moving on to the first proper consonant, the same rule applies. Whilst it is not really possible to hold on to the 'th' sound for any longer than a split second, I have heard singers elongate the sound a little too much, pushing more air through their lips than is really necessary. So, sound the 'th' clearly and concisely, but get *off* it as quickly as possible, and form the 'i' vowel,

Now we reach the 'nk' sound at the end of the word 'think'. This is interesting, because immediately afterwards we have the word 'I' again.

The question is, *where* do we place the 'nk' sound? You might think that it should (obviously) go at the end of the word 'think'. However, that thought process does tend to 'end' or 'cut' a musical phrase, by it's very nature.

In fact, you should **place** the 'nk' sound ON the word 'I' itself.

So, instead of singing, "think I", you should actually really sing, "thi-nkI." As such, the 'nk' sound acts as a springboard into the "I", rather than the 'nk' sound cutting the line.

The same happens at the end of the line, with the last two words, "love you." The 've' and the 'y' sound should be placed together. That is NOT to say that you try and sound the 've' and the 'y' at exactly the same moment, creating a kind of 'vee' sound.

Rather, you sing the 've' sound and then, immediately afterwards, you sing the 'y' sound, with no gap at all. This creates a compound consonant. This involves two consonants (or sometimes more), which are squashed together. One is sounded *immediately* after the other, so that they take up no more time on the musical line than they have to. That then allows you to get straight back on with the glorious process of singing the open, musical vowels.

As you can see, vowels are king. Having said that, you should not regard the consonants simply as a servant to that king. Consonants should always be clear, clean, crisp and precise. However, a singer who consistently holds onto consonants for an unhealthy length of time will never sing as well as the singer who realises that open vowels are the tools with which they can demonstrate the power and beauty of the voice.

Of course, there will be times that you do actually need to break the legato vocal line, but this is usually for dramatic effect. For example, a singer might decide to sing, "I think.... I love you." As such, the gap between 'think' and 'I' is placed for dramatic effect, perhaps because the singer is having doubts about the character they are singing to (in other words, "I think I love you... but I'm not entirely sure"). Or they are concerned with the reaction that character might have hearing this news; in other words, "I know I love you, but I'm concerned you might react badly to this news, so I won't be quite so forceful with my feelings at first."

Making musical 'sense' of that line

You are now aware that all vocal lines should be delivered smoothly, unless the music calls for something else. You do not want to sing in a disjointed, staccato-like way, and the advice given above, whereby you should concentrate upon joining up the line of vowels, is the best way to create a legato line when singing.

However, we must then 'make sense' of that musical line.

Too often I have met musicians who think that 'give it more of a sense of line' and 'make musical sense of the line' are the same thing. In other words, they simply think it means, 'Sing more smoothly!'

They are, however, two different things.

'Give it more line' does indeed indicate that you should be singing more smoothly.

But 'make more sense of the line' actually means something else. It is, in fact, what you do **to** the legato line *whilst* you are singing. It is the impetus, the musical stresses, and drive behind that legato line which make musical and dramatic *sense* of it.

The analogy I use is this: I like driving. I prefer the countryside, as I find motorways boring. The national speed limit is 60 miles an hour, and there is nothing I like more than driving around the open road of the countryside at this speed.

However, my joy is often ruined by someone driving at a consistent speed of 35 – 40 mph. And there is usually no place to pass. So I sit behind them, frustrated at their lack of progress. Then, we may reach a village, where the speed limit is often 20 mph.

I consider myself to be a good driver and, as such, I slow right down to 20 mph.

But what does the driver in front of me do? Carries on at 40 mph. They often seem to have little self-awareness at all regarding other road users or the highway code in general.

If you were to draw the 'bad' driver's speed on a graph, what would it look like? It would be an almost straight line.

However, a good driver will tend to speed up, slow down, speed up, slow down, and usually, when they are getting close to their destination, they will probably be going their fastest on account of the fact that they 'just wanna get there!'

If you were to draw the 'good' driver's speed on a graph, what would that look like? Naturally, it would have peaks and troughs. It would rise and fall.

Now, if you take the 'good' driver's graph, and apply it to the legato line, but rather than thinking of it in terms of acceleration, think of it in terms of volume, drive and impetus; this will make the musical line far more interesting.

Sing a legato line all at one volume (like the bad driver) and you will sound like a robot. Sing the legato line with variations in dynamics, and the line will come alive dramatically.

I teach a number of actors in the West End, and I find that they are masters of adding drama to the legato line. Some add a little too much (and end up with a line that is a little choppy in nature) and I find I have to draw their attention back to the legato line itself. But it is far more interesting to listen to this than someone who sings the line in a robotic way.

Some singing teachers describe this process as being like a fast train that roars through a station, taken from the point of view of a passenger standing on the platform. The sound rises, reaches a crescendo, and then diminishes. However, that is a little too general for my liking.

For example, you may have to hold a long note for several bars. Again, do you just sing it at one volume? No! A good singer will 'shape' the note. In other words, they will probably start it quite quietly, and then grow in volume. They can then either build to a crescendo, if a 'big finish' is required, or they can bring the volume back down again towards the end, depending upon what is expected musically.

In all cases, these analogies, when understood, followed and applied to the legato line will help to make musical *sense* of that line. They will also make dramatic sense of the line, enabling your audience to understand more of what it is that you are trying to get across in the song.

All these tips and tricks will help to bring your singing alive, and pull you away from being just another average singer.

Chapter 11 - Choosing Repertoire

EVERY DAY, NEW SONGS are written.

Old ones comes back into fashion, whilst others that have been popular tend to fade for a while.

As such, writing a huge list of songs for your consideration would be unwise, as it would be out of date within a short period of time. Indeed, the subject is so broad, an updated list of songs would actually require its own book, updated on a yearly basis.

However, I wanted to include a few of my own thoughts regarding the songs that you choose.

Essentially, unless you are doing graded exams, you should dictate the songs you choose to sing. Your teacher should also have ideas, based upon the choices you make. If you find that your teacher simply rehashes the same old songs, week after week, month after month, find a new teacher.

Of course, some of the best singing teachers do not always play the piano. In this case, you may wish to pay for a pianist to play for your lessons.

Your teacher may use backing tracks, and that's perfectly acceptable, although I have always been grateful that I trained as a pianist first, as having to pause and rewind recordings is always a waste of lesson time, and can be imprecise.

If you have no idea at all about what you want to sing, I would suggest trying everything that appeals to you.

Most of the time, singing students are generally attracted to the type of repertoire that they feel suits them.

Occasionally they get it wrong. I had a student who, for a few weeks, brought an anthology of George Michael songs. I played piano for him and he attempted, against my advice, to sing them. He would then get very cross with himself, as he consistently missed the high notes. The truth of the matter was that he was a baritone, and the songs were just too high for him.

"I don't understand it," he would say. "When I am at home, singing along with George, everything sounds great."

Of course, when he was at home, what he was actually hearing, first and foremost, was George Michael and his band. Of *course* it sounded good! What he wasn't listening to as much was the sound he was actually making himself. And, when the high notes came around, I am sure that George 'covered' most of those for my student.

When he then attended his lessons with me, all that 'support' via George and his band was taken away, and he was left rather exposed with just my piano.

So be careful what you choose. Of course, everyone wants to be the next George Michael, or Beyonce, or Pavarotti or whomever you admire. However, it is important to choose repertoire that shows you off, not up.

I have had several students in the past whose voice 'types' have not suited their chosen profession. Some have clearly been destined for the musical theatre stage, but have pushed themselves towards pop, without success. Others have been on the professional music theatre stage, when they were clearly more suited for pop.

Some have come saying that they wanted to sing jazz, but have actually ended up able to sing classical.

And very occasionally, you get a singer who can do it all, and do it convincingly. These types turn up once every ten years or so.

Record yourself. Listen to the timbre of your voice. Does it really suit classical? Or would it be better suited for heavy metal? Be honest with yourself, and your musical career will go further.

I once worked with a singer who sincerely believed he was destined for the rock industry, singing in a band. As time progressed, it became clear however that the voice was not right, and he is now studying opera at the Royal Academy of Music. Very different indeed.

It can take time to work out which musical genre your voice belongs to. These days, the boundaries are not *quite* as tight as they were. Classical crossover has enabled some of our greatest classical musicians to branch out into a more commercial world. However, it has also allowed some rogues to exploit the general public. Whilst I believe people are entitled to love whatever music they like, it is important to understand the difference between a proper, bonafide opera singer, who has spent years on the professional operatic stage, playing many roles, and a classical singer who simply did some training at college, had certain surgical enhancements and then thrust themselves into the limelight.

So, in conclusion, work out what genre suits your voice best. As you do so, remember that this will dictate the musical world you then inhabit.

Most of all, make sure you enjoy it. After all, that is why you and I chose music in the first place.

Chapter 12 - Final Thoughts

I HOPE THAT THIS BOOK has gone some way towards dispelling the myths regarding singing and vocal tuition.

I sincerely hope that it has not further confused you, but rather has explained a number of questions you may have had pertaining to singing, but were afraid to ask.

I simply ask one thing; please do not rely upon this book solely to teach you the art of singing. It won't work. Rather, employ the services of a great singing teacher, and use this as your reference guide. And in this day and age of Zoom and the like, you do not even need to live in the same country as your teacher. I now teach students all over the world, mainly online.

Not only should your singing teacher refer to most (if not all) of the techniques mentioned in this book, they should embellish and extemporise upon them also.

Simply reading about vocal technique and then doing little about it is about as much use as reading a book on exercise but never going to the gym.

Great singing requires serious study, and even the greats spend a lot of time on their vocal prowess. How else do you think they became great?!

Time and dedication will always pay dividends, and I can assure you that, having placed hundreds if not thousands of singers through the method described in this book, they have all ended up singing better.

And that is all a good singing teacher should do; help his or her students to sing better.

I sincerely hope you find a great teacher.

Wishing you good vocal health.

Sean Jay MMus GGSMD

For further enquiries, email: singingtutorpro@gmail.com

Don't miss out!

Visit the website below and you can sign up to receive emails whenever Sean Jay publishes a new book. There's no charge and no obligation.

https://books2read.com/r/B-A-KEJEB-QVLYC

BOOKS 2 READ

Connecting independent readers to independent writers.